If There Were Roads

○ ○ ○

If There Were Roads

o o o

poems

Joanna Lilley

TURNSTONE PRESS

If There Were Roads
copyright © Joanna Lilley 2017

Turnstone Press
Artspace Building
206-100 Arthur Street
Winnipeg, MB
R3B 1H3 Canada
www.TurnstonePress.com

MIX
Paper from
responsible sources
FSC® C004071

Turnstone Press gratefully acknowledges the assistance of the Canada Council for the Arts, the Manitoba Arts Council, the Government of Canada through the Canada Book Fund, and the Province of Manitoba through the Book Publishing Tax Credit and the Book Publisher Marketing Assistance Program.

Printed and bound in Canada.

Library and Archives Canada Cataloguing in Publication

Lilley, Joanna, 1967-, author
    If there were roads / Joanna Lilley.

Poems.
Issued in print and electronic formats.
ISBN 978-0-88801-607-2 (softcover).--ISBN 978-0-88801-608-9(EPUB).
--ISBN 978-0-88801-609-6 (Kindle).--ISBN 978-0-88801-610-2 (PDF)

    I. Title.

PS8623 I43 I3 2017   C811'.6   C2016-908177-X
                                                C2016-908178-8

In memory of my sister, Rebecca Lilley,
and our mother, Patricia Lilley.

Contents

We Are the Creatures / 3

Stepping off the Bus

The Devonian Period / 7
St. Gennys Church / 9
Sassenach / 11
Bryn Gwynant / 12
Two Ghosts / 14
Bluebird / 16
Hike / 19
Summer Sleep / 21
The Third Coast / 22
Crossings / 23
Stepping off the Bus / 25
Falling in Sheer Snow / 26
Chapel / 27
Ten Mile Cabin / 28
Not the Moon / 30

Hand to Mouth

The Bather / 35
Grandfather / 36
Watching Television / 38
Waterlogged / 39
Hand to Mouth / 40
Charity / 41
Just a Man / 42
Bare-faced / 43
Unhinging the Jaw / 44

Felled / 45
Grief / 46
England / 47

Interspecies Engineering

The Gamekeeper / 51
Country Life / 52
The Abattoir Worker's Wife / 54
Burns Supper / 56
Horses at Knockdarroch / 57
Thief / 58
Idling / 59
At the Aquarium / 60
Sacred Cow / 62
Behind the Houses / 63
Microchip 958 000 000 411 618 / 64
Night Vision / 66

Invasive Species

I Blame the Parents / 69
Set to Silent / 71
Turban / 72
Tea Ladies / 73
The Film Director / 74
Cookery Class / 76
We Are in the Clouds / 77
Skid Row / 78
Rainier Avenue / 80
North Klondike Highway / 82
Canada Day / 84
Potsherd / 86
Aloysius / 88

Coming to My Senses

Poet's Stone / 91
Craflwyn Hall / 92
No Land for Standing / 94
Rosie in Her Red Coat / 95
Them / 96
Certainty / 97
Pot Luck / 98
Seventy-Two Hours / 99
Leaving the House / 101
Folding / 102
Waiting for My Husband / 103
Dreaming, or Awake / 104
You Will Not Die / 105
Hope Stone I / 106
Hope Stone II / 107
Coming to My Senses / 108

The Stones of Torphichen

The Stones of Torphichen / 113
Home / 115
Tinto / 116
Where I Was Born / 118

Notes / 119
Acknowledgements / 121

If There Were Roads

o o o

We Are the Creatures

, , ,

We are the creatures who build new homes of sticks around
our old homes so we can live in two places at once. We are
the creatures who travel to other countries carefully, carrying
the geometry of all our shelters and all our people. We are the
creatures who remember each of our dwellings wherever we
are, even if we've sloughed off our skins, cracked our shells
from our backs, and cut out the brands burnt into us. We keep
moving all our lives, never going so far that we cannot return.
We remember the first rooms we slept in and the beings who
slept close by. We know the bodies of our origins. We mind
them always and deeply and still.

Stepping off the Bus

○ ○ ○

The Devonian Period

. . .

A house can divide into flats,
multiply into an old people's home,
flower into a shop, change more than the family
who used to live there. It can disappear.
Trees or flats can grow in the gap.
Hedges rise and façades can be repainted,
so you can't always be sure when you visit
on Google Earth, standing in the road,

staring for as long as you like without
worrying about a curtain moving
or someone coming along the pavement
with bags of shopping to ask
if they can help you.
You don't have to decide
whether you want to be invited in.

Google Earth takes the photographs
you didn't. Three women walking past
the gate, the laburnum in yellow flower,
two children, bare-armed, one in red trousers,
one in green, nearing Mrs Harrison's window.
She gave you Mint Cracknel when
she had some, money when she didn't.
Your mother, Hoovering, found the coins
you hid under the carpet.
She gave them back on your behalf.

Google can't take the picture from
your bedroom window, the notch in the sky
you watched each summer night,
a granite hill with a snag of a church on top,
built by a merchant saved at sea.
You didn't know what a ley line was.
You're still not sure, except you know
it's as strong as steel, tensile
as spider thread. You can still feel
the cool white paint of the window ledge
under your elbows as you rested
your chin in your hands, wondering
how long it would take to cycle up there,
if there were roads.

St. Gennys Church
, , ,

The coastal path plummets.
The wind pushes your father
over as we descend. We sit
him damply down
and break him off a row
of his own chocolate.
Scoops of sea spill
snow on the beach.
There's more weather
at the top of the cliff,
all over the grass.
You take your father's arm.
I list the England I miss:
bladed cow-green grass,
tubular yard-broom grass,
dark sea anemone grass,
the scent of gorse's coconut
as a blackbird dashes.
There's a secret beach near here
my parents led us to each summer.

Hailstones break our stride,
bend us from the sea.
We cross the muddied, sloping
field up to a church.
Your father won't enter,
or even shelter in the porch.
He stays by the gate in the rain,
hood up, a broad hand
bracing the wall. Inside
the empty church,

the rain is silent.
Stone combs the arches.
The vaulted ceiling breathes
through darkened ribs.
The greenstone feels warmer
than the granite.
Gripping the shoulder
of a pew is how I withstand
the undertow—the urgent
tug to sit and stay.

Sassenach

> ○ ○ ○

Standing on shingle with her back to the southern city, she's
whistling chilling tunes to freeze the sea so she can walk across
it. Age eighteen, she's too old for pubs and clubs. She sees
photographs of bens and firths and applies to university in
Edinburgh. Finds a room with a view of the capital's paradox,
Arthur's Seat. But however hard she blows she can't inflate
the atrophied lungs behind Samson's rocky ribs and revive a
350-million-year-old volcano. Unable to inhale the city, she
leaves before it exhales her, urban lava lapping at her feet.
Driving north, she's jealous of the car; its tyres pressing ground
while her backside only hovers, sealed in city-air she packed
along with her clothes and flask of coffee. Needing a job, she
tries to stop in Inverness but the car has acquired the taste of
Tarmac, licks the road until it's all gone. Standing on the beach,
her back to the land, she daren't look round.

Bryn Gwynant

∘ ∘ ∘

A place I left twice,
the first time knowing,
as I drove across the moors
to Capel Curig, I was leaving
Wales too soon. That was June.
In January, I was back,

making beds, cleaning loos
so I could walk up Snowdon
in an afternoon, run down
for a swim in Llyn Gwynant
before my next shift at five.
Or walk slowly between gowns

of rhododendrons, intruders
like me in that sodden valley,
suffocating the ground
with their skirts, sweeping
even worms from lightless soil.
A single summer crop

of lavish purple flowers
from commandeered earth.
I snapped the curving, top-heavy stems,
put them in beer glasses for vases,
petals dropping soon.
I threw spent blossoms

onto the summer fire, pushing open
the wide wooden door to reap
a new clutch of conquering blooms,
cramming colour into my cottage
before the fading autumn of paling grass,
rusting bracken, and three-day rain

cleared to a shock of summit snow.
I knew I had to leave again,
return to England, enrol at college
so I could find a job that paid
in more than rampant rhododendron
leaves gleaming in the rain.

Two Ghosts

. . .

A brown-clothed figure, human, a man,
knees bending as he moves up the hill
towards late sunrise. He doesn't see me.

A farmhand on his way to work
a century ago. I see him briefly;
he's not there when I look again.

This farmhouse in the Perthshire hills
is fixed above a valley I could live in.
Behind me there's a rainbow,

one end planted in the nearest field.
It's so close I could run to it,
not caring it wouldn't be there

when I arrived. I stay
and wait for the others. We walk
up the muddy lane the way

the farmhand went, listening
to the burn, leaving the track
to traverse a field of tussock grass

to a high point where we can see
Ben Vrackie, the mountain
we will climb tomorrow.

Dusk comes later when we get back
home to Canada. I walk
with our husky in the woods

below a light blue sky, a blurry moon.
The wind has stopped. I feel her soft
moist nose push at my hand.

She usually hangs back, waits for me
to step aside so she can pass.
Hunger must be making her hurry.

I look behind: she's ten metres
back, between two spruces.
It wasn't her.

I'm not scared by these stitchings
of then to now, these malfunctions
of skin and eye.

They are as natural as when I see
the moon and the sun
at the same time in the sky.

Bluebird

o o o

My boyfriend had a vision:
my bicycle chucked in a truck;
It would be red, he said.
As if he'd ever been to Canada.

A man I served at the bar asked
if I was going still, now the desert war
was on. I should carry a gun, another said.
As if he'd ever been to Canada.

It was twenty years ago today, the day
I started. A long bicycle ride,
drawing corners on a ragged country,
I stretched six thousand miles

to fit in enough aloneness
after all the cram of England.
Len the long-haul trucker saw me twice
on his trans-Canada run.

The third time, he came out of a café
as I went in. Fourth run, he bought me supper
at a truck stop. A salad, for a vegetarian,
with jelly and marshmallows.

He'd got out of Keeseekoose, saved
for a semi that cost more than a house
and made it a home. He hadn't seen
his daughter for half her six-year life,

didn't know if he still had a wife.
Len said I shouldn't camp. He offered
me his bunk. We slept beside each other
after he got back ache on the front seat

and asked to share. When I left, he gave
me a song on a dirty, cracked cassette.
Anne Murray's *Bluebird*.
Not my thing but beautiful.

He said he meant it. That was Saskatchewan.
Chester in Nova Scotia had seen me too.
He made me pancakes. Marc in New Brunswick
took me home for apple pie.

He told me he had a girlfriend.
Ray—Ontario—kept giving me food,
said I must eat as I cycled along. I left
the helmet he gave me in a campground.

Women didn't feed me.
Alice in Ontario said she was jealous:
all that time to think. Marianne
cried because I was on my own.

In Manitoba, Judy the teacher caught
me camping at the school.
I slept in her white house
down by the sunken Birdtail River,

a riddle of hills that were really the prairie
above. Helen in Alberta called me
a fellow traveller, told me the bird I'd heard
since Quebec was just a wood thrush.

It wasn't supposed to be about the people.
It was the land I wanted: skies, the muskeg,
taiga, the bear who crossed the highway,
the coyote who followed me, the foxes

who watched. In the Yukon, Julie
took me to her cabin on the Dempster.
It took me fifteen years to make it back.
As if I could live anywhere but Canada.

Hike

, , ,

A hoary marmot sounded a warning whistle
as four of us dodged the grassy hummocks
on Mount Decoeli's slopes—a football referee
stopping play, reminding us to pause and look.

As we lunched, the marmots ran like low red foxes
through the forget-me-nots to crouch
at their burrows under bear-proof slabs
patched with orange lichen. We crept too close,

crushing purple harebells and yellow-dotted
avens to see two blades of teeth, shaggy shoulders,
and get our pictures. The sheep ignored us
and the marmots' whistles, staying to graze

far from our path. Ascending, I gripped rocks
with all my weight, forgetting to test them first,
as if I'd never hiked before. We didn't keep together.
Sue knew a better route and crossed a snow patch

to a gully. Jim, her husband, had to follow.
You and I went straight up to save time.
The pyramid of shale was sharp, scoring our boots.
Every step, our feet slipped. We caused landslides,

trickles of stones sliding like geological water.
Sue and Jim got to the summit first. At the top,
we smiled, took photographs in the rain, then put
our cameras away to watch for glimpses of ridges

and peaks in the clashing clouds. Descending
all together, we foot-skied down the snow,
sometimes surfing on our backsides, even
on the shale. Shards skidded hard behind me,

cracking my ankle bones. We followed
a broad, bouldered stream back down the valley
and missed the path. Our map was rubbish
and no one had packed spare batteries for the GPS.

We forded a mossy river in our boots, up to our knees.
We twisted through thickening spruce and yellow
Arnica flowers, too tired to talk of remedies
for bruises. We listened for the highway,

walking in shadow under a band of evening gold.
The road, when we found it, was hard and grey
and welcome. The rhythm of our thudding
boots paced us back to the car. Keys in my grip,

I looked back at Decoeli's perfect summit,
now bare and sharp against blue sky.
I'm glad it cut and bruised us. I'm glad
we didn't have a clear, clean view.

We're not meant to find mountains easy.
We're not meant to go wherever we like.

Summer Sleep

. . .

She is not a summer being; she is
a species whose metabolism slows
at solstices of heat and drought. June
was cooler than May, July is hotter.
August will be her inferno. She will
keep herself from cities, open every
window and close the blinds.
She will stay in her basement where
the clay behind the wall is cool and damp.
By September, she will have left her arid
home and husband and boarded a bus
to the coast to find an island. Beneath
a plaited cedar, she will lie on shadowed
soil and push the sun away with palms
of green and glossy leaves. She will
plant what's dry—her heels, her elbows,
her mind—and leave them while she takes
a swim, checking each time she comes
up for air that they're still there.

The Third Coast

° ° °

It took two nights, two days of aspens,
spruces, to reach Churchill by train.
I had a day; I couldn't afford to stay.
All I wanted was to touch and taste the sea.
The rusting sign on the way to the beach
said there were polar bears. I didn't take
my shoes and socks off; I quickly crouched
and dipped and touched cold fingers to my lips:
the sea was brackish, diluted by melting ice.

I sat in a white, wooden church while the noise
of a tour group left. Their guide waited at the door
for me. I explained I wasn't in his group.
He sat me at the front of his bus regardless,
pretending not to hear me say I had no money.
The bus drove over snowless tundra, felling
Arctic willow, neutering lichen. We stopped
to watch three polar bears: a mother
shouldering her cubs. Two Spanish men
lent me their binoculars. I saw the shadow
on the mother's muzzle, her grubby teeth.

The Spaniards were small and as beautiful as birds.
They were going to a tundra cabin, far from town,
with cameras, pencils, and paints.
I wanted to watch white bears from a window
with them. My bed that night was a seat
on the evening train. I sat for two days
going south again, trying to draw dark noses,
broad paws, a taste of wild white sea breath
on my tongue.

Crossings

. . .

I

At minus twenty chocolate doesn't taste of much, even if she
tongues it against the roof of her mouth. This low-horizoned
place, she sees, is where the sky comes for a rest, letting the
tundra take its weight. She's been looking at it on the map for
years, the Arctic Circle round its knees, fingers reaching for the
North Pole. The countries stitched together by a circumpolar
thread, she's going to every one of them. She wants to stand on
the flange of ice at each end of the rod that skewers the Earth,
fixing one pole to the other. She snaps and sucks another
square of chocolate. When she's done, she's going south to sail
the ice desert's watery rampart, the Antarctic current; perhaps
she'll observe how chocolate tastes down there.

II

First stop inside the Arctic Circle, she steps from the train. No
one else gets off, no one embarks. It's later than it looks. No use
for towns, she walks, a backpack-tilted giant. Willow, spruce,
birch: small trees, small leaves for a small summer. Northern
paucity enriches; southern abundance wearies; she's tired of
lying on beaches. Removing sunglasses, she dares the sun to
touch the horizon. It won't. Rolling out her sleeping bag on
crow and cloud berry, she grips her knees, watching for wolves
and bears. Within an hour, she returns to the station, unrolls
again; lies on the platform, seven hours early for the next train.
Perhaps reindeer will dip their muzzles as she sleeps, warm her
with nostril-breath. Her eyes remain unshut, sky-sheeted. All
night it's as if she's watching some other planet's sun.

III

Sixty-six degrees, he says, thirty-three minutes, thirty-nine
seconds. Parking, he tells her to take his camera, goes to the
back of his van. Don't look, he orders. When she does, he's
high-kneeing into black trousers. When she looks again he's
tuxedoed. In the tundra. Hold this. A friend, back in LA, he
says. A composer. An in-joke or she's missing something. Just
for fun. It's a baton, white for a dark concert hall. Here, black
would show up better. There is so much light, white dissolves
into brighter sky. A man in a tuxedo, arms raised to conduct a
symphony in gold and red of folded mountain, unfolded plain.
He is orchestrating light and space, not music. The only sound
is the wind. It doesn't matter that she doesn't get it; she snaps
his photo.

Stepping off the Bus

° ° °

I got off the bus too early in the dark;
I was engrossed in Lorna Crozier.
The bus driver opened the doors.
I was off, on snow, before I realized
I could have said sorry and stayed on.
Farther to walk to work at minus thirty,
past the paddle steamer in the park,
dry-docked for decades.
The glow of snow before late dawn,
the wide, flat, static river.

I remembered the woman
commuting on the bus
from Bathgate to Edinburgh
who woke in the dark,
temple resting on cold glass,
and couldn't remember
if she was on her way to work
or going home.

Falling in Sheer Snow

. . .

The ski pole has you in a half-Nelson,
painless. You drop backwards
between spruce shafts.

Snow fixes you, wedges your widest parts.
You didn't grow up with snow angels
watching over you.

Snow was an unreliable element,
never staying. Your head looks up
at the thick blue sky you are in,

the human tantrum.
You spend hours in this forest
that ends days away. Close up,

a stopped gush of waxy yellow sap.
Farther, smooth gold aspens shoot.
All you see now are tree stalks

in the snow. These are your roots,
your only grip on the Earth.
You grab a tawny spruce trunk

sideways,
grasp rough, dusty bark,
a taste your tongue can't articulate.

Chapel

, , ,

Walking through the chapel
of leafless aspens, I sometimes
remember to turn, to stop before
the snowy slope to the creek
with the toothpick bridge the dog
tiptoes across. I am inside an oval
seed. I raise my arm-wings, tilt
to an almond sky, an eye,
standing in a nothing,
a wintered shape of air.

Ten Mile Cabin

◦ ◦ ◦

I felt a bit like that too, the dog,
wanting to be told what to do
while trees were being timbered,
hauled through snow to the jetty.
One limbing. One standing
on the trunk while another sawed.
I fathomed a job for myself eventually;
I pulled the logs up from the lake
to the cabin in the plastic pulk,
the dog coming up and down
with me, both of us slipping
in the same spot. Every time.

Later, in the dark in a bunk,
giving up on the wood stove,
swaddled in my thick, fat
sleeping bag, I lay on my back,
eyes in a bundle of body.
I recollected oblivious, umbilical
warmth, a mass of comfort,
when nothing was upside down,
not even me.

Skiing ten miles home
on white rises sloping back
to level fields, or lakes.
We couldn't tell.
Everything was constant, broad:
the snow, the sun, the sky.
I kept stopping
to take my hat off
so I could hear the silence better.

Not the Moon

. . .

It's dark again, walking the dog at six,
always our forest triangle so I never
have to think which way to go.
Passing possible wolves, I make

myself practise a presentation.
Startled by the creak of a tree,
I rehearse with squirrels
office conversations

I'd rather have by email,
if at all, thumb to-do lists
on gloved fingers because my pen
won't work in the cold.

Pencils set my teeth on edge
at every temperature. If I get
outside before the work thoughts stir,
I listen to ice silencing the creek,

feel the burden of blood in my hands
and feet, think how soles stay softer
than our palms all our lives,
though pounded perpetually.

Before this winter's snow fell
to light my way, walking
in the rooted dark I tripped
and wrenched my back.

I gave in to diurnality and switched
my headlamp on, the dog's eyes
flashing discs of alien green
when she checked back for me.

I aimed the beam at squirrel height,
glanced up to find the moon. I was sure
the moon was shining, though the sky
was as dark and solid as a cave.

It was not the moon in my peripheral
vision; it was the headlamp gleaming
on its own silver rim. I switched it off.
I'm sick of tricks of eye and mind.

Hand to Mouth

o o o

The Bather

。 。 。

Wiping inside my mother's fixed, folded hand
with a soft, damp flannel, I feel the frame
of her immobile tendons, the dented cushions
of her fingertips, the silk of unused skin.

I wind and swing her from the bath, wrap her
in towels my father hung on the radiator to warm.
With her left hand, the only one that works, she levers
the fingers of the lifeless right so I can cut her nails.

She bends her fingers back too far. I'm the one
who winces. I have bathed my mother
for longer than she bathed me, though not
as often; I am almost always away.

I am as familiar with her body perhaps
as she was with mine. The slender strength
of her working thigh, the skin tag by one breast,
the tiny triangles of nail on her little toes.

Her back is waxy now, swimming muscles
fused to her shoulder blades. Everywhere
we lived, she took me swimming. Dark
dragonfly rivers, shallow splashing rivers,

always the sea. She knew when I was ready
for my first mile in a pool. I can't recall learning
how to swim; she carried me into the water
as a baby, holding me with two working hands.

Grandfather

. . .

He left an arm by the silty Somme,
one of the million men
who were the capital raised to buy
three French miles short of nine.
He was lucky it was his left.

Or lucky his mother made him
right-handed so he could comb vinyl
grooves in his oiled hair until
he was ninety-two. Or ninety-something.
Only three of us remember he was born

in eighteen-ninety-eight.
There's no one now who could pick out
his mother in a photograph.
The ink on the back is fading.
He had ten siblings. Another war rifted them.

Grandfather set his alarm for war too early.
His plans to be a clockmaker dropped
by the young hand that was buried in France
with the boy corpses. Square-nailed,
gall-knuckled, only his right hand came of age.

After the Great War invention of trench watches,
wrist watches were all the rage. He had no
spare fingers to strap one to his single wrist.
He wore a pocket watch instead,
a timepiece marking his survival,

thumbed into the fob pocket of the moss
waistcoat he wore for the long rest of his life.
He earned his living sorting letters,
the alphabet his gut line, shuffling addresses
deftly with one full set of fingers.

He used a paperweight to write his own.
At least he could keep chickens, wringing
their necks one-handed. He salted his food
before he tasted it every time, adding
angina pills to the tablets for black-outs.

He made it to ninety-two,
or was it ninety-three, died sitting up
in bed on four firm pillows, his pocket watch
still ticking on his night table,
his loose pyjama arm tucked neatly in.

Watching Television

° ° °

I had breast cancer before I had breasts,
watching a grown-up television programme,
sitting on the blue hearth rug, the paraffin heater
scorching a stripe on one side of my face.
I sat with my back against my mother's armchair
as she pushed a knife with the length of her thumb
through a spotted Granny Smith, a chunk
of farmhouse cheddar, a slice of fruitcake.
She cut and watched, forgot to send me to bed.
Lying later in my room, pressing two hard discs
inside my flat chest, I knew I was going to die.
The television programme said lumps
were how you knew the cancer had come.
I never told my mother. I never told my friends.
I only told my cat, my rock, my tree.
I checked every night, after my mother's kiss.
The lumps didn't grow; breasts did.

Waterlogged

, , ,

The body in the sea at Elie
was hers. Long black t-shirt
dragged waterlogged towards soft
pale knees. She'd driven for an hour
to find a place no one would know her,
yesterday's pizza on the passenger seat.
The heat that summer drove her
to outside water, the only element
in which her atoms dare let go.

The next weekend her body
sought the deepest hot loop
of the River Avon. Beyond
the beech grove she uncovered
her skin under sticky leaves
and damselflies. She would
spin in the open every day if she
could hatch out of this body.

She used to think sleeping
was a waste of time, now
she wastes more time awake,
waiting for her fingers to give in.
She is the unnatural animal who
detests the vessel that carries her,
who yearns to be less than herself.
There's a desire line in her mind,
a shortcut to the lie she tells her body,
that they will die together.

Hand to Mouth

○ ○ ○

Her fingers are heavy on her hand,
her bones wrenched by the heft
of flesh.

Her hips are ramparts moated
by moon pull, her fat-lagged liver
dank and bitter. She is a case against
cannibalism.

In England, lying in bed, pubescent,
she shoves her stomach under
her ribs, scoops her thighs back onto
the mattress.

In France, self-taught at fourteen, her fingers
reclaim the novelty of hunger over a sink,
sunlight between the shutters warm on the back
of her neck.

In Greece, she sees a goat tethered
to a stone-fixed stake. She hears a clang
and the short, taut rope of four decades
slackens.

The life she has wasted despairing,
busy-mouthed. She has hung joy at the back
of the wardrobe. She is earth where grass
has worn away.

She was once a bee, a tiny light bee.

Charity

...

Her midriff records each year. Hope, solidified, layers her navel, folding as she bends to tie up another bin liner of clothes that no longer fit. She lifts the sack into her car at night and sets it down at dawn outside the children's charity shop. Last time, it was the shop for the elderly; she alternates causes according to which flowers first: regret or fear. Disappointment, she knows, might not ripen to failure if she waters it with hope. She draws a picture of a watering can on a Post-It note and sticks it on the fridge.

Just a Man

. . .

I wish I could be just a man
passing by a row of shops.

A man as ordinary as a road with potholes,
as a bridge across a river frilled with brown foam,

or the tugboats of a working firth.
A man where urban is normal,

where a park is unremarkable,
where dogs walk without pulling

and pigeons peck at screwed up burger wrappers.
I wish I was a man in a jacket, collar down,

a little fashion in my trouser leg, passing by
a doorway, a yellow skip, a litter bin,

past men and women at the bus stop
who barely notice me.

I wish I didn't care that the sun has set,
that the street lights have come on,

creating shadows,
and I'm still half a mile from home.

Bare-faced

o o o

She needs large skin
to smear her self back on
each morning after a shower,
smoothing it with her lifeline,
her fingertips, twisting her hand
to reach between her shoulder blades
which are not the nubs of atavistic wings.
They're the bones that will be most
ambiguous when unearthed,
collapsed onto shifted ribs.
She is a woman in all the right places,
a man everywhere else.
She is brazen, bare-faced.

Unhinging the Jaw

◦ ◦ ◦

A body, lying pillow-faced in bed,
may scream at the end of every day
of ghastly human doing, dying
each night to sleep.
The sound will spasm, lock-jawed.
The legs will jerk to the cold
edges of the sheet. If
shriek remains unhatched,
tadpoled in a moorland pool
where grass floats like hair
in a bath, the tendrils of a yawn
will rise inside a closed-mouthed
cavern, unhinging the jaw.
If it never gets past the teeth,
the screech will come to work,
to desk, to dinner. Swallowed,
it will hatch, nose into blood,
into lungs. It will split each breath,
hacking molecules, fill
the lungs with incarcerated carbon
until the mouth at last opens
on the bus, the train, the plane
and there are a hundred
witnesses to the spread-eagling
of the sternum, the bare
and bloodied stillness of the heart.

Felled

° ° °

My head aches and I wonder
if it's the shock of the cold.
All these coats to puff in the dryer,
hankies Velcroed to cuffs,
fleece legs with socks inside.

I'm not dead yet,
there's just something stuck
between my shoulder blades,
like the axe in the log outside,
waiting for a horror film to be made with it,
arching me constantly,
as if I'm felled.

Grief
॰ ॰ ॰

Eyelash, when it dropped, collected.
Cat claw sheath, sloughed,
enveloped inside a date.
A white whisker shucked,
resting in the jewellery box
with the stiff, invisible drawer.
I never found a black one.

~

I type out what actually happened
each letter by heavy letter:
what I know, not what I didn't do
or should have done.

~

When I feel sick with the turning,
instead of looking down
at the roundabout, I fix
my sight to spruce, to aspen,
flip my head when I spin,
like a ballerina, like a sailor
hitched to the horizon.

~

I've stolen seven pebbles from the lake,
a circle garden for the Zen calendar
on my desk, needing roughness
knocking in my grip, needing Earth indoors.

England

。。。

My father will cut an apple with a blunt blade.
My mother will arrange sultanas around
the rim of her plate.

Her signature is a left-handed circle.
My father stopped her adding large kisses
when she signed her pension book, with regrets.

The radio will be off in case we talk.

I will walk back from the station
the long way round along the seafront
to avoid the dark streets mostly

because they're too familiar.
Pellets of foam will shoot off the hectic waves.
I won't be the only one to wonder

if Hurricane Sandy is changing course.

The pink carpet in the bedroom
that was never really mine will still be soft
under the palms of my feet.

A fortnight of mist is nearly over.
I am more here than there now.
At home, do fingernails really crack in the cold?

(Shutting the door of the train to Gatwick
will be hardest, the momentum of slam,
the smell of dusty seats.)

In the morning, I will listen to my father
take my mother a cup of tea,
tap the spoon to wake her melodically.

'Obama won,' I will hear him say.

Interspecies Engineering

· · ·

The Gamekeeper

> > >

This far north, midsummer nights are frayed,
unravelling to reveal more light than is decent.
At three, the gamekeeper wakes to brighter
than usual light. Rolling from his wife,

rising to the window, he stares as flakes fall.
This numbing snow is rare in June, though
bar and beer-glass rumoured. Outside, his boots
break crystals as he strides to higher ground.

Red wattles quiver. He cracks a frozen bog,
walking watchfully, slowing through heavy stalks.
He bends to scoop a dappled grouse chick
to his cheek to feel for heat and breath.

There are many corpses stored in heather caves,
robbed of a summer life he would have granted
in preparation for a more glorious August end.
A skyward soar, plummeted by a gun,

soft bodies rushed five hundred miles to London
to be plucked, drawn, and roasted the same day.
He folds his fingers over the chick. He presses
until he hears the click and snap of fracture.

Young bone breaks so much more easily than old.
A harrier, high and silent, glides towards the heather.
The gamekeeper walks away across the moor.
Today, he'll let the creature cannibalise its kind.

Country Life

◦ ◦ ◦

Flip on your cap, whistle the dog.
Kiss me goodbye, mouth open.

Why won't you share your English
country ways with me?

If you reach the beeches without
looking back, I'm going to follow you.

Your little dog knows I'm here, though
she's not telling. We walk for fifteen minutes

to a sudden mossy stop. I hide behind an oak
as a stand of flat-capped men surround you.

Dusk loudens sounds as mist magnifies
mountains. A few human words set off

the yapping. Terriers sniff at holes.
Larger dogs stay back as men grip shovels.

Men yip, the terriers go down.
I hear a frantic subterranean squeal.

A screech and your dog is out,
muzzle ripped back from sticky teeth.

You reach past your screaming dog
to tug at a bulky body, shabby-furred.

You raise your spade, crack it down
on the badger's black-and-white striped crown.

I'm clamped by the stench of musk and blood.
I'll never open my mouth for you again.

The Abattoir Worker's Wife

، ، ،

At the abattoir, the workers switch off
the throat cutters and reach to unclasp
the feet of the chickens hanging upside
down. Some of the birds die at the touch
of warm broad hands.

The worker on his break puts down
his ham sandwich, lifts eight birds into
a crate that held eighty when they came in.
He drives home slowly, braking
gently at traffic lights.

His wife, who made his sandwiches,
is out when he gets home.
She's taken the pig from the fridge
to bury in the cemetery. He carries
the crate carefully into the house.

His knees crack as he crouches to invite
the chickens onto the living room
carpet. When his wife returns,
they decide to give them
the spare room for now.

They spread newspaper sheets on the floor,
fill margarine tubs with water.
She takes them sunflower seeds
she finds in a kitchen cupboard
then goes back downstairs for a cup of tea.

They agree it's quite nice black.
He isn't sure if they will have to pay
for the operations to relieve the pain
of shorn off beaks and broken wings.
She says if they do, they'll find the money.

They discuss how many cows
could fit in the backyard. The abattoir
worker wonders about sheep.
His wife smiles. She says
she's always wanted a lamb.

Burns Supper
. . .

Every year on Burns Night,
my heart was broken by a shining haggis.
Cleaned, scalded, soaked, and salted
before it was baked. Addressed, fingered,

sliced, gutted, and digested afterwards
by people of surprisingly diverse
political persuasions in one room.
I leaned on one thick soundproofing palm

to protect at least one eardrum from the
barrage that piped the inside-out stomach in.
I preferred the blast of bagpipes far and high
on a Glen Coe hill. Indoors, they were the mace

that stunned the lamb who gave its heart and lungs.
Onions, oatmeal, coriander, nutmeg.
It must have happened: a lamb's organs minced and sewn,
thick-threaded, inside its own mother's stomach.

Horses at Knockdarroch

, , ,

After a curry last night we parked
the Fiesta beside two of them
in the dark. Outside animals. Quiet.
Horses, standing massive in the morning.

Through the skyless window in this rented
bedroom only snow, firs, fences, grass,
until I sit low on the painted window seat,
see clouds flattening billows of pink mist,

as if they're trying to pack up a tent.
If I understood how horses stand the cold
I might know why humans save them
for riding instead of eating, because

cows stand in the dark by cars too.
Now a girl in jodhpurs gets out of Daddy's
green Range Rover. He leaves her
in the paddock beyond the field.

I watch her walk the largest horse in wide
circles, imagining my back broadening,
spine thickening, fingers fusing into hooves,
waiting for the weight of leathered cow.

Thief

。。。

He likes the scrape of stone on skin as he climbs cold granite.
Enjoys the pull of muscle and tendon after seated hours of
driving. Too heavy, he snaps a birch branch. Looking up, no
shallow wingbeats are returning deep-chested parents to their
ledge; their circlings and stoops are not for him. In the hand,
one egg looks too small. To have driven this far, climbed this
high. It's easy to reach for the other three. *Falco peregrinus* will
be back next year to breed again; all he will cause is brief con-
fusion. The drive home is quick and slow as congratulation and
anticipation pair. At home, the final work is done. The needle
slides in, holing shell and membrane—both ends—to release a
summer smell of egg. He blows the gluey dribbling insides out
and flushes them down a toilet. He arranges the cases on velvet
beside last year's batch, a heavier, riper crop when it had not
been as easy to expel the lives inside, when he had poured acid
into a larger wiggled hole to dissolve the downy contents.
A flesh smell then, not egg.

Idling

∘ ∘ ∘

On the way to the bus stop
I pass a pick-up truck at the mall
with a moose rack on the back,
wishboned by its skull,
a cheap black chain looped
through one eye socket.

A khaki ball cap is on the dash.
The truck is red and idling.
Hunters say they respect the animal
they're about to shoot.
It takes guts to respect what's left:
unfastened, enduring bones.

At the Aquarium

. . .

Perhaps all the people streaming past
make Pacific herring think they're moving,
balled in a perpetual shoal
inside a lidded cylinder,
a giant jar of silver spinning fish.

Over children's heads and hands,
above the spikes of their voices,
I watch one herring flow contrarily,
nose up until it divides into purple bubbles,
a dark eye drifting out of its own light.

The whole shoal changes direction as I watch,
though I don't see it. I was observing
how only the back third of each fish moves.
There's plenty of space around this core of sea.
I can't get past the sound of them.

You're showing me the five-hearted hagfish
down on the fake sea bed, sliding
into a dead fish's anus
like a turd pushing the wrong way,
to eat it from the inside.

You remind me to be thankful for the hagfish
And—your favourite—the Sexton beetle:
the waste disposer and the undertaker.
I look back at the herring trap, still hearing
the dizzy cram of the eternally shoaled.

A man and boy eat chips from a plastic tray
in front of the Quadra Island tank. In front
of Australia, two parents crouch to double
phone-snap their children glassed and laughing
at spitting White-barred Gobies.

In the Amazon rainforest
I grab the finger of a Cecropia leaf.
There's no glass. I don't move
when water drips on my head.
A perfect ibis shadow tiptoes across the wall.

Sloths—dark burls above us—eat vegetables.
They take at least a week to digest a meal.
In the Strait of Georgia, the label back there said,
herrings' eggs are caught on blades of kelp and eaten.
When we leave, I avoid the jar of fish.

On the bus I hear them still, squashed
in that cylinder, sick with endless circling.
But when I Google Pacific herrings,
it says they live in shoals all their lives,
so all I'm hearing is water stirred in a glass.

Sacred Cow

o o o

A fortnight after you get home,
adopt a black dog from the shelter.
Keep forgetting to post a donation

to the bona fide Indian animal charity
you found after the effort of three emails.
It would be so much easier through PayPal.

You know that white dog you saw
is dead by now. Remember the cow tied
to the railings on Sasmira Road in Mumbai,

the old lady crouching on the pavement
beside a pile of grass,
the businessman

who stopped to buy a handful,
who fed the cow,
and went home blessed.

Behind the Houses

. . .

On the dam, big and fat and slithery,
round and gorgeous. I saw her before
the dog did, before she saw me.

She backed up on the glistening sticks
and twigs and logs and leaves and took
time turning and splashing into her pond,

swimming with her head out of slippery
water darkened by baggy clouds. The
slapping splash of another beaver sliding

from the far bank got the dog's attention
and we ran together, across the flooded
footbridge, splattering along the track

that was dry yesterday and now was a beach
for the one-way tide of a rising lake. They
were supposed to be dead; my neighbour

told me the city had killed them because
they were clogging the creek. Perhaps
the city won't notice this woody causeway.

I won't tell them. We can build a higher
footbridge to cross the swelling water.
We can build a jetty for our canoes.

We'll amalgamate our infrastructure
with theirs: a feat of interspecies engineering.

Microchip 958 000 000 411 618

∘ ∘ ∘

I

About the size of a long grain of rice,
the microchip lies by a spruce needle
under an aspen leaf,
delivered to the forest floor
inside a twisted defecation that was soft
before it was hard, whitened, desiccated.
The fur in the scat no longer orange,
more the colour of frayed rope.

At the back of the cat's neck
between the shoulder blades
on the dorsal midline
is where the microchip was inserted,
injected by a vet in Scotland,
from there by air to Canada.

Bioglass passes smoothly
through a coyote's digestive system.
Chip, core, capacitor intact, uncracked.
Or it may have fallen in the seizing, ripping.
I may pass it each day with the dog,
unscanned.

II

The coyote who ate the microchip
may have been eaten by a wolf.
Or a raven may have eaten the coyote's remains,
flying the microchip farther into the forest. Or
the raven, standing on top of a lamppost
gurgling and plunking, might excrete the microchip
to the road where, say, a Honda Civic runs it over,
presses it, whole, into the pavement,
soft on a hot day. The road re-surfaced
a few years later, the microchip
sedimented in landfill,
eventually excavated by a future race,
human or otherwise.

Night Vision

. . .

Through the back gate,
two pairs of eyes in the flashlight,
fox-height, not coyote,
between spruces, side by side,
still as stars. Hand on
the dog's back. Let's not.
Coyote-height, not fox.

Back through the gate,
round the road to the woods.
Two pairs of eyes electric
in the flashlight,
fox-height, or coyote.
We've all shifted, halted
in a different triangulation.

Invisible creatures standing
on leaves and needles.
The dog's eyes are on me.
Will we walk tonight
between the wide eyes
of boreal creatures? Not
coyotes, not foxes, not wolves.

Invasive Species

o o o

I Blame the Parents

, , ,

Actually I blame the child
for making the telephone call
across the terrible Atlantic
from Florida of all places,
land of heat and beaches,
Mickey Mouse melodrama.
Not religious conversion.

Her mother on a green telephone,
falling to her knees in the hall.
Her daughter calling to say
she wasn't coming back to England;
she had a world to save.
It took only a few conversations
in small rooms to give her mind away.

It took only three months for her
to forget about seasons, flying back
to Gatwick from Florida bare-legged.
It was February; there was snow.
Her poor little mind,
still a fontanelle at eighteen.

Her parents took her to Venice
to fill the Florida gap with Europe.
They left her alone in the Arena Chapel,
trusted her to return to them on the lido.
The chapel sky was perfect blue.
She gazed while her mother swam
in the Adriatic, waiting for Giotto
to paint her daughter's mind back in.

Set to Silent

, , ,

Travelling, she once wore underwear for three days;
her bra and underpants wouldn't count as dirty until
she arrived and took them off.

Commuting, she sits on the train in clean
underwear each day. She should read
her book instead of watching people playing

Angry Birds on their mobiles. At least
they're set to silent. She's worried the dexterity
passengers practise daily on the train will make them

evolutionarily superior to her. She prefers to read;
all her fingers do is hold a book and turn the pages.
She doesn't even like crosswords. No one else

seems to notice the graffiti comic strip the train
passes every day on a warehouse wall right by
the tracks. So far, the train has gone too fast for her

to read it. The graffiti artist didn't think of that.
All she sees is a hippy teacher in a classroom.
She plans to catch one word each time she passes:

she's got to three so far. *Let's, start, again.*
She hopes the effort will be worth it; she hopes
the comic strip will make her laugh aloud.

Turban

◦ ◦ ◦

On a British Airways aeroplane to Delhi,
the knees of the old man behind me
poke my back. He's mumbling or praying.
The steward has told him twice to be quiet.
I was in the middle of watching
The Kids Are All Right
when his turban tumbled down
on top of me,
opening his tenth gate
and closing mine.

Tea Ladies

◦ ◦ ◦

Headscarved women submerged
to their chests in clouds of fields
are lopping glinting pekoe leaves
with box contraptions, scooping
them into sacks on their backs.
At the top of the track, other
women sit on the ground outside
the factory, puddled by their skirts,
sorting bad leaves from good.
A man stands watching. Another,
arms folded, leans against
the flimsy corrugated factory wall.
Inside, leaves are laid on the floor
to wither. Tea dust wedges in cracked
window webs. In the rolling room,
the crusher has *Lanarkshire Steel*
embossed on its side. The workers
who made this Scottish steel might
have drunk this tea on their breaks,
dunking Tunnock's wafers in their mugs,
before their industry dissolved.

The Film Director

๐ ๐ ๐

This is the quietest India they've found,
floating to sea-silted islands where poverty
is painted purple, orange, green.
If only the guide would stop talking.
His wife's shoulder is dappled by sunlight
through the banana hat that scrapes his ear
each time she twists to look.

There's a man at each end of the boat,
pushing a pole. The film director tells them
they're *gondolieri*; they don't get it.
There's a boy on the bank, waving,
calling hello in English. He's eight, perhaps.
A blood red tilak on his forehead. Now
he's speaking Malayalam or Hindi,

holding out his hands. He has bracelets
on each wrist. Red shorts. His belly button
protrudes. The film director's wife remembers
reading about packing pens to give to children.
He tells her, no, Kerala has the highest
literacy rate in India: ninety-four per cent.
These people don't need pens.

His wife is a producer. She won't work
with him because they're married.
The boy is still on the bank, smiling.
The film director touches the pen
in his shirt pocket. He got it in Milan.
It writes so smoothly, almost worth
the price. It's his autograph pen,

just in case. The boy has hundreds of pens,
for sure, in a box behind the curtain where
he sleeps. The film director sighs and slides
the pen from his pocket. He throws it
carefully over thick, black water. The boy
is good at catching. Of course he is.
He knows the English for thank you.

Of course he does.
The film director's wife squeezes his arm.
They pass a floating flower. He reaches.
The guide says it's an invasive species.
The water is so warm it doesn't feel wet.
His wife smiles as he eases the flower
into her hat.

Cookery Class

° ° °

The teacher gives me a shallot to chew, purple-tipped and
sweet. It's not the spices, it's the Keralan air making me wheeze
as if a wet flannel is sucked to my mouth. The teacher leaves
the kitchen to take a call on her mobile. Her assistant sits on
the white-tiled floor, cross-legged. She calls him Boy. He must
be forty, forty-five. We look down on him from our chairs. He
grates a scoop of coconut, black-knuckled. He doesn't look at
us; I'm smiling in case he does. He's quieter than the parrot
in the garage whose beak reminds me I must cut my toenails.
The teacher comes back and drops a dollop of masala on her
flat palm, tastes it with the point of her slick tongue. She is a
good boss, she tells me after the lesson, as she cuts up fruit
for the parrot. She lets Boy visit his wife and daughters once a
month. They live four hours away. The teacher is solid, smooth
and golden. Her orange salwar kameez glows. She stands so
proudly as she slices mango, her feet apart, her stomach out.

We Are in the Clouds

∘ ∘ ∘

In this aeroplane, I sit across
from a boy playing a computer game,
a girl reading the Bible. This is human
life capsuled. I'm watching tiny films.
My transatlantic record is five.

I pause the screen and slide the blind to look.
There is nothing human about clouds.
No faces in them or mythological creatures,
castles. No species, no gender, no kind.
Only roiling, rising, vapourising.

A cloudless sky is not a blessing,
it is a cloudless sky. Yet weather lifts our dust:
the skin cells we perpetually shed.
Our dust sticks with ice and salt to cooling droplets,
making water visible.

Skid Row

...

The monster freeway lying on the waterfront is dying.
This disintegrating, dirty, double-level concrete
has a shocking glamour, a future monument
to automobiles, more worship-worthy than a view
of Olympian mountains across sun-ironed water.

It's twenty years since I last leaned my forearms
on this scratchy cement wall in the Pike Place maze,
glaring down on the droning freeway, counting
juddering drivers with no passengers.
They're still gushing by. My heart's not in it;

the world will have to save itself. I flip around.
I'm near First Avenue. I want to see the cheap
Skid Row hotel I stayed in after three days
on a Greyhound bus, where men sat soft-legged
on their beds, their doors wide open

as if they'd just come out of prison. Where
cockroaches skidded their carapaces under
my locked door. This is it, I'm sure. So now
it's glassy, glossy restaurants, plants in and out,
Patagonia, Quiksilver sparkling across the street.

The pizza bar's gone too. The pizza guys
were good to me. A free fungi four-cheese
for my first post-teenage birthday, a beauty
gift certificate I would have wanted now.
They tried to fly me to the Sunshine State,

a bonus birthday gift, if I'd haul a package to Miami.
Instead, I took a bus to view a room in Wallingford.
The owner gave me tea and homemade oatmeal cookies.
No need for a deposit, she said, if I promised
not to go back to Skid Row. No, not even for my luggage.

I never returned to see the pizza guys.
Yet this is where I've come to gaze today,
to this gentrified street with chunks of ocean
down steep intersections, where I can stand
and listen to the freeway dying.

Rainier Avenue

. . .

The night above the blinking planes is dense as soil,
reminding me of where I've come from.
Slim people play tennis under bright sodium lights
as I trek to the Safeway I was told is down this street.

Cars shush and whisper as they go downhill, bicker going up.
Gruff buses flick away a clatter after they've passed by.
The sidewalks are empty beyond the tennis courts.
Bare walls, sharp shadows, torsos of pollarded maples.

At last, the Safeway sign. It's nearly ten
when I start back along a silent street.
Carrying groceries, I'll look local. I used to march,
pretend I had friends just up the road

when I was somewhere new, out late.
Tonight, I'll summon mobile magic.
I turn my cell phone on and hold it
to my ear to talk to no one.

The first man I pass finds out *I forgot the cheese.*
The next man gets a film review
and *I don't know if I'll have time this week,*
I've got a major deadline.

The ground-floor apartment where I'm staying
has too many windows. I swizzle all the blinds
and draw the curtains. I switch on a table lamp
to fortify the corner. I check each closet,

behind the shower curtain, double lock the door again.
I leave the living room lamp on when I get into bed.
I never needed a nightlight as a child.
I never closed the curtains.

I'm not afraid of the dark
back home in the woods.
I don't bother with a flashlight.
In boreal night I am invisible.

North Klondike Highway
° ° °

Travellers push open their camper doors,
stand tamping dust, not sure why
they've stopped. They're not hungry.
There's nowhere to top up the gas.

They've been staring for hours over soft,
disappointing hills, watching for a rip
of mountains below the sun's slow bounce.
Some stroll to the middle of the highway

to stop astride coagulated yellow lines
and memorize how a road looks empty.
The shabby store in a cleft of shining forest
draws them all, not the thick, broad

river they think they'll see again.
By the time they're in the store they're
in the mood for microwaving and pouring
bottle coffee. The open-lidded creamer,

spilt like laundry powder on the counter,
reminds them they need to find a laundromat.
The handle of the suction fridge quietens them
like a soother. It could be time to try iced tea.

Sour cream and onion Lay's between their knees,
pistachios dashboard dancing,
they don't look back when they drive off.
They didn't think of living here;

they didn't see the village in the bushes.
They don't imagine snow and minus thirty.
Yet they know now where they are;
they're not looking for the mountains any more.

Canada Day
. . .

It's lunchtime. I'm almost Canadian.
Arctic Rangers in red hoodies muster
for a photograph on a knoll while we wait
for the citizenship ceremony to start.

They wear khaki camouflage trousers, though
there's snow here more than half the year.
That—and the red—they want to be seen
on the tundra, signify Arctic sovereignty.

My MP, a Tory and a cage fighter,
tells us in English how big Canada is,
as if we chose the second largest
country in the world by accident.

We have to swear allegiance now
to a queen I'd vote to overthrow. I mumble
other words. The gesture is hypocritical;
I've already signed the oath on paper.

A Malaysian boy plays beside me,
dropping sweet wrappers on the grass.
I glare at his tired father who carries
a smaller boy; he doesn't catch my eye.

As soon as the speeches stop,
I tell the boy to pick up his litter.
I'm ready to insist.
He collects the wrappers immediately,

bending narrow knees, swinging slender
fingers to the ground, as if dropping
and picking up are unconnected.
Between certificates and handshakes,

I watch the father take a nappy from
a bag hooked to his buggy. He gives it
to a Swiss woman whose child is crying.
Afterwards, my Canadian friends come up

to hug me. They say congratulations.
Laura tells me it's a really big deal. Yet
I've kept my British citizenship. It's like
having my fingers crossed behind my back.

Potsherd
For Victoria

, , ,

There is nothing here in my frontier garden
so far from England to remind me of you.
Guilt is an actual heaviness, the weight
of china fragments in the blood,
blunted each time they pass through
the heart machinery, yet catching still.

It was easy not to arrange for time off work,
book a train ticket, find somewhere
to stay in London for a funeral,
easy to be too busy, to make
the living more important than the dead.
It was easy to send a bad poem instead.

I wrote that you were like the sherds
of blue and white pottery I found
in my garden when I made mud pies.
As if a childhood image equalled
my body by your coffin. You knew broken
things had sharp edges, could be used

to slice open, look inside. You had scars.
You were almost accident-prone. You
slipped on your icy front doorstep.
Your back was always going.
You knew the order of things. A church
wedding when you were thirty,

you had your babies afterwards.
I think you sometimes believed in heaven.
I'd rather not go to work today;
I want to sit here at the edge of the forest,
on the peeling deck in a green chair,
early, before the mosquitoes come.

Aloysius
o o o

The passenger beside me on the plane
from Vancouver to Toronto
held a teddy bear on her lap
the whole five-hour flight.
I think she was a woman.
Her face could go either way,
dark-cheeked with acne on both sides.
She wore a black and white knitted hat,
a padded coat and snow boots,
though the only snow I saw
was high below us in the Rockies.
Taking off, I could tell she was
eccentric like Sebastian and his Aloysius.
It occurred to me over Manitoba
she had brought the bear as a pillow,
though she never put it behind her head.
As we descended to Toronto,
she bent to hug the bear so tightly
I realized she was terrified of flying;
she needed childhood comfort.
She kept her hunched grip while we taxied,
even when the door clunked open,
which was when I wondered if she'd landed
where she couldn't be: dry-eyed,
as we all must be eventually,
even grieving for a child.

Coming to My Senses

○ ○ ○

Poet's Stone

, , ,

Leaving the pub, striding up
the steepest road in Wales,
we overshot the hostel;
we couldn't bear to go indoors.
We walked until we found the starlit
poet's stone, built where neolithic
ground rises. A foot and hand up to its roof
where we could sit, confess
our invisibles, swap the parcels
of our started lives in the lunar dark,
high above the gentle Conwy Valley.
It took the moon and Drambuie
for you to speak.
It took you for me to kiss.

Craflwyn Hall

◦ ◦ ◦

The house came with your summer job,
downriver from me and the hill fort
King Vortigen tried to build by a dragon pool.
His men laid down their tools each night
and every morning found them gone
and all their walls dismantled.

You had the house and all its contents
to yourself. Liver-spotted photographs
tight in envelopes. Dulled oils in tarnished
gold leaf frames. Ink in marbled ledgers
too faded to read. Mouldered hardback
books bequeathing sneezes.

Every room smelled of damp clothes
left in a washing machine. A squirrel kept
scratching at the kitchen window, scoring
tiny, mudded marks. Ceiling grease mapped
the fat fryer. The dust was finger-printed.
She hadn't long been dead.

I'd never not opened doors before,
nor gone halfway upstairs in daylight
and turned back down. You slept there
once alone and did not sleep. You heard
tables, wardrobes dragged across the floor
upstairs and hoped it was the plumbing.

The next night I cycled from my place
to lie awake with you on the sagging bed.
You didn't need to ask. When I got up
at three to go to loo, the silent, empty hall
was noisy, crowded. I couldn't find
the light switches. In the morning, a pen

on the kitchen counter had definitely moved.
Your boss found you another house
to live in where you were the only occupant.
Craflwyn Hall is a guest house now;
the lounges *retain their historic character.*
I wonder who survived the renovation.

We've never been back to Craflwyn.
One day we'll go. We'll book a room,
trace squirrel scratches on the kitchen window,
ascend the hill to look for crumbled stone.
At night we'll check the light switches.
We'll dream of dragons when at last we sleep.

No Land for Standing

o o o

A week after our wedding
you gripped the gabbro of Cuillin ridge
for seven miles, climbing

each black pinnacle,
lugging food and water for two days.
There were no burns that high.

I stayed at home, not trained for ropes
and toe-holds, sitting on the floor
where I felt safer.

A decade later we stand at Turner's
elemental scraping, looking at a face
of stone and tempest. I know Turner.

I like to think I knew rock, air, and water
were one thing before I ever saw his pictures.
He's teaching me again.

I don't speak while you look.
A spark of rock leaps through cloud,
stone sucks water. This is no land for standing.

You tell me now you weren't skilled enough
for that climb. Staring at that dash of loch,
you didn't know you'd make it home.

Rosie in Her Red Coat

◦ ◦ ◦

Rosie in her red coat drove all the way
from London to see us in our cosy cottage
up a grassy slope with views of Snowdon,

where we would live forever,
or at least all summer,
while we both had jobs.

Rosie, her red coat on the newel post,
waited for us to rise. We were knackered
from our shifts at the Llywelyn Arms.

Rosie, her red coat bright on the green hill,
strode far beyond us. We panted to reach the top.
Rosie said she ran each day in Regent's Park.

Rosie knew how to live in cities,
how to get a proper job that paid, how to save
for years to purchase property to rent

to people like us who can't afford
the grown-up life, renting now
Rosie's little fifth-floor flat looking down

on stumps and squirls of pollarded
plane trees, a second-hand street,
and a bookmark of park.

Them

. . .

I
Her beam is narrow.
She shines it on details
for hours, seldom
sweeps it side to side
to work out where she is.
His beam is broad and bright.
He sees everything at once.
Sometimes he wonders
why she's squinting.
Her beam might blanch
the night eyes of a forest fox.
His would warn ships off rocks.

II
He wants river glitter in his eyes,
sunshine all the time,
a star shower, if it has to be night.
He wants happy rain, warm sea,
bubbles on his computer screen
whenever he stops working.
He's the cat lying tummy up on the warm deck,
She's the dog lying belly down on cool earth.

Certainty

He has so much of it,
swelling like the iced creek
that smothers the footbridge
she crosses each day, sometimes twice,
with the dog, watching for slips.
He never considers that she might leave him,
that she doesn't tell him everything any more.
Spring is edging. Ice could still lever
this bridge from its place,
could still unslat its purpose.
This bloated opaque turquoise
on which she and the dog stand will melt.
It will shrink each day the sun
stays longer above the boreal curve.

Pot Luck

。 。 。

She sits beside him, on the soft couch
with a mug of tepid tea,
the ginger tingling, as her neurons do
from his stubble, cropped hair, bright eyes,
from sitting close. The look, his smile,
the bantered words that aren't meant exactly,
they're surely efforts to say he thinks she's
wonderful. She wishes, she wishes she
could slip her children off for a little while,
leave them lying at her feet on the floorboards,
something else she never does—she never
does. She will keep her children on, of course,
and, on top of them, her husband across the room.
Yet she will never take this tingling off, the warming
layer when she walks tomorrow in minus one along
a broad pale river where smoothed stones
are glacial in a city too far from mountains.

Seventy-Two Hours

. . .

Four crescendos of wind
in the light night,
a solid shatter of sound.
A nuclear suck of poplars
through the blinds.
The house unbroken for now.
I lie back down beside you.
The cat lies back down on me.
You say the cat keeps you awake
but I can hear you snoring.
I am used to loving weather,
not being afraid of land
liquefying, of a river gorging
on kitchen cabinets, of lightning
hotwiring the toaster,
charging the fire break.

The cat's tail twitches to
the rain on the tin roof.
You stop snoring.
The dog folds in the corner.
In the morning, I must
remember to print the list
for the seventy-two-hour
emergency kit. Buy a large
bag from Canadian Tire.
Put the cat carrier in the house.

Once the bag is ready,
I will tape to it a list
of what to grab on the run
to the car: the dog,
the cat, my laptop,
your accordion, you.

Leaving the House

° ° °

The house must be awake when we
leave each morning, not faking.
The house must not waste the day.
The blinds must be horizontal
to collect more dust.
The closets closed, the iron
cooling. The house must be
the order we leave behind.
The radio must be dumb,
though we never ask the dog
if she'd prefer it on.
The dishes exiled. The loo seat
down, or up for the cat
in case we never come home;
the alarm clock re-set,
an amulet to ensure we will.

My husband waits in the car,
his laptop on the seat beside him
that he moves when I get in.
I hand him his sandwiches
filled with morning sex.
He would let the house sleep in,
disorder being proof of life in progress.
I don't want him to help me
shake the house awake.
As I bend to tie my shoelaces
in the footwell, he turns the ignition.
Reversing out of the garage,
he says, *I'm coming with you
for the CT scan.*

Folding

° ° °

When the telephone rings, I clamp
the receiver between my shoulder and ear
and line up the edges of a discarded napkin.
Listening to the radio news, I concertina
a Home Hardware receipt. I iron handkerchiefs
into hot triangles. I set the wood stove
with folded fans of newsprint. Cat hairs
glide across the waxed oak floor,
the bathroom mirror is blotched.
I stand at the kitchen window and fold
a yellow tea towel until it is as small as you
once were. I find it on the windowsill
later, as I watch a waxwing eating
mountain ash berries, sprinkling snow.

Waiting for My Husband

. . .

He is half a baked potato left
to eat cold the next day.
He is the kitchen sponge
with too much water in it.
He is the finger sliding,
checking email. He is
the vinegar I forgot to pour
into the kettle to clean it.
I put on thick socks and cross
my legs on the couch, remembering
skinny Cher in Moonstruck, eating
as much ice cream as she liked.
The branches don't scrape the tin roof
since my husband borrowed
the neighbour's clippers.
The squirrel doesn't scratch
in the attic since he blocked the soffits.
A fruit fly soars past the screen
in silence. The only sound
is my fingers tapping keys.

Dreaming, or Awake

o o o

I watched the stars last night;
now the sky is dark again.
The stars were smaller, duller,
as if the Big Bang were pulling them away.

The dog had a twisting fit last night.
I held her in my arms. I woke to her nose
before I knew I was dreaming.
The hollows in her eye-bones

are real, her slow-hipped conquer
of the couch, though she's only three.
The bad haircut I gave myself is real,
a teenage mistake at forty.

A visit to a hairdresser
is two lines of a vet's bill. A drive
to town is time for tummy-rubbing.
The stars are fixed; Earth falls.

You Will Not Die

, , ,

You will not die with bear spray in one hand
but with a harmonica you will blow wheezily.
Our friends will not call to offer me help,
sit with me through light nights,
ask me if I'm going back to England.
I will not have to make those phone calls.
You will not make the local headlines for two,
three years. There will be no coroner's
recommendations, no court case.
Helicopters will not hurt you.
Helicopters will not find you.
I will keep you until you are shorter,
until your hairline rises
and you think my glasses are yours.
You will stay with me until your hearing
is as bad as mine. I will listen to you play
until I've made up words to sing.
I will lie in bed dreaming to the tempo
of your snoring. I will lie in bed believing
one day you will be older than me.

Hope Stone I

。。。

There is a stone behind my house
I took five years to see.
I found it walking the dog late
in my dressing gown and rubber boots,
going off the path so no one would see me.
I waited for permission to sit
on the ancient lichen aureoles.
The dog sat beside me, stilled,
listening as I watched the flashing creek
through rickety aspens collapsed
against a grey and orange sunset.

The top of the stone was flattish.
I placed there the chill of the woman
who died on Everest, the autumn
of the Arab Spring, the perplexity
of Iraqi refugees on their way
to Canada, the shrieks of shelved,
impounded chickens I hear perpetually.
Last night, near the stone, the dog found
half a rotted rubber ball. She took it home,
through the trees, through the back gate
into the garden. I let her carry it into the house,
grateful for a house, a garden, a gate, a wood,
a creek, a stone to lay things on.

Hope Stone II

° ° °

The hope stone is the guard stone,
the release stone to the ten stones.
The ten stones of my grief, of
what else are my hands to do
except pick up stones.
The striped stone, the candle stone,
the stove stone, the bathroom stones.
Smooth upstairs, rough downstairs.
The stair stones where we sat.
Each stone lined up along the porch
after ten days of searching
for a dead cat in the woods.
For ten days, it rained. Each stone
I put down wet changed colour overnight.

Coming to My Senses

. . .

This house is made of honey logs.
If the carpenter ants weren't eating it, I would.
Four of us live here. My husband

who mostly forgives me for not cooking.
A dog who can't bark.
A cat who would rather live in Mexico.

I lock all four of us in each night, after
I've hidden the saws and axes. I keep
the windows dirty deliberately.

The sea, I miss it.
I dip my hands in up to the cooling suicide line
each time I cross the creek.

I'm watching the prairie crocuses die
as the Jacob's Ladder flowers.
I tear off sage when I walk up to the look-out.

After I sniff, I put it in my pocket.
Once I took some all the way to England
by accident. I sprinkled it on the pavement

outside my parents' house to bless it.
The dog lies down if I look at the view too long.
They're the best part of me, my senses.

I cry each time I hear an ambulance,
even though my mother and my father
both came back. I cry when crowds

of people sing or shout together.
I forgot again today to give back more
than I took. Kissing the cat should count.

The Stones of Torphichen

o o o

The Stones of Torphichen

, , ,

I
Hermit

It was for their quietest brother that St. Fechan's monks heaved
Torphichen's glacial stones to build a beehive clochan. High
on the crags he crouched, nipping rosehips, skinning rodents,
wrapping bracken round his toes, mortaring his rocky cell
with moss at cold dusk and plucking it out with guilt at cooler
dawn. Until his body began to die before it was grown; lying,
dying, stroking ivy's gloss. Waiting for the raven's dark beak to
bleed his flesh and pick his soul from his bones, to carry it to a
heavenly nest where rest need never be clandestine.

II
Architect

They rolled the stones down from the crags and knuckles,
down from the hill forts and the burial grounds to form a cross
where safety would be granted: a kirk the torso, the fields and
woods the arms. They left the marked stone on the windiest
summit, at Scotland's narrow waist, rolling only its broken
abdomen down to stake the sanctuary's core. St. Ninian,
building his fragile wooden kirk beside that central refuge
stone, admired the strength and permanence of rock. Once
home, beyond the westward hills and forests, he resolved to
build an entire church from such eternal matter.

III
Preacher

High on the slopes of Witchcraig, the preacher climbed the
boulder to face his outdoor congregation. Barred from the
kirk, he whispered thanks for his airy words, the magpie's
interruptions, and the raven's gaze. Louder, he praised
Craigmailing Farm for his pulpit, keeping his eyes from
Cairnpapple's rounded height and his mind from adding to
his collection. Each time he trod the little summit, he filled his
pocket with stones, as if to weigh himself down on earth, not
ready yet for God's embrace. At home, warming granite with
his clutch, he wished he could lie in the hill's deep cists, his
finished body insisting on decay.

Home

...

I softly press the tiny mosses
rebounding green each boreal year.
I dip my finger in a clump
of crystal snow, small as my boot,
that will be gone tomorrow.

Tinto

. . .

How a hill matters
watched from a train,
looking up from a book,
coming home from London,
sitting on the right side to see
the shining shallow Clyde,

cut like peat from the grassy
moors beyond the Uplands,
before the falls, before the port.
We walked once from our house
to Tinto, along pink lanes,
up the quiet side,

the prehistoric heave of a lone hill.
I went up on my own sometimes.
Living in the woods, needing
barren mass, an effort of height.
With you, eating cheese
and Marmite sandwiches at the top,

backs to the wind, settling
our bottoms on clunking stones,
imagining Ireland, Lochnagar.
It's Scotland's largest cairn,
as old as smelting. I wish I'd known
we were supposed to carry a rock

to the top each time. Instead
of bringing, I took a Tinto stone.
It lies here now on my sill in Canada,
where I live in the woods again.
One day I'll return it to its cairn,
put Scotland back where it belongs.

Where I Was Born

° ° °

I am not just from where I was born;
I am from where I've lived.
On Dartmoor's sheep-cropped edges,
beside golden, bouldered tors.
A shingle beach, a chalky sea,
a lane to a preceptory.
A valley, waterfall, a cairn.
And, yes, that first rough field
of shaggy grass in Cambridgeshire
my parents brought me home to.
A brown pond, a thatched roof
over a weak floor, a sheepdog
watching my pram. For I was born
within the sound of horses' hooves,
across the county line in Suffolk,
farthest from the Bow Bells
of the litter. My siblings
can have their London births.
My first breath yanked sheets of air
from fens as far as sea, from roofs
with spaces in between.
I have sought those spaces ever since
and found them even in the boughs
of plane trees on a city street.
They stay with me, these spaces.
I've brought them here to the forest edge,
where land might still be sacred.
Though far from field and moor and sea,
I am at last where I need to be.

Notes

The Devonian Period
Hoovering means vacuuming in colloquial British English, after
the brand name. Mint Cracknel is a 1970s British candy bar.

Sassenach
Sassenach is a Scottish term for an English person. It's derog-
atory but not entirely for English people use it too, a little
tongue-in-cheek.

Grief
A roundabout is a British word for a merry-go-round (rather
than a traffic circle).

Tea Ladies
Tunnock's wafers must be eaten to be truly understood. They're
a Scottish chocolate, caramel, cookie bar.

Aloysius
Sebastian is a character in Evelyn Waugh's novel *Brideshead
Revisited*. Sebastian is grown up but carries his teddy bear, Aloy-
sius, everywhere he goes.

Potsherd
This poem is in memory of Victoria Browning.

No Land for Standing
Gabbro is an igneous rock, similar to basalt. Burns, in Scotland,
are streams or creeks.

The Stones of Torphichen
I lived in Torphichen, a village in West Lothian, Scotland, from
1998 to 2006. Jack Smith's booklet, Torphichen (1997), educated
me about the anthropological, religious, and spiritual signifi-
cance of my surroundings.

Hermit
Hermit monks are said to have settled in the Torphichen area
in the fifth century, living in isolated, cone-shaped huts made
entirely of stone (called clochans). One such clochan, known as
the grotto, was across the road, through the woods, and over the
crags from my house.

Architect
Torphichen was known as a place of sanctuary that extended for
about one Scots mile in each direction from a central sanctuary
stone in the kirkyard (churchyard) that may have originated at
the pre-Christian burial site of Cairnpapple nearby. The early
Christian missionary, Saint Ninian, is likely to have recognized
the importance of the sanctuary stone. He was born in 362 and
built a timber church on the site of what is now the Torphichen
Preceptory. He also established what is said to be Scotland's first
stone church, in Whithorn, Galloway.

Preacher
In 1690, the Scottish Parliament abolished the right of lairds
(Scottish estate landowners) to choose ministers for their local
churches. When the new British Parliament reversed this deci-
sion early in the eighteenth century, the Torphichen congrega-
tion locked the minister that their laird had chosen out of the
kirk (church) and instead followed the minister they wanted to
hear out into the fields where he preached to them from a boul-
der still known as the Preacher's Stone.

Acknowledgements

Thank you to my parents for getting me into the habit of moving from an early age and for always encouraging me to explore. Because of them, I've lived in beautiful places and am grateful that those places continue to live in me.

This book and I have been on the road for a long time. I am indebted to Sharon, Jamis, and Sarah at Turnstone Press for pulling over and giving me a lift all the way to the destination I was dreaming of reaching.

I have had much help with these poems en route. Early on, Maureen Hynes put up signposts and guided me with kindness and encouragement. The Sage Hill Poetry Colloquium was a revitalizing rest stop I could have lingered at for much longer. Thank you Ken Babstock, Kristina Bresnen, Heidi Greco, Katherine Lawrence, and Mitch Spray. Dave Margoshes finally charted the way for these poems to become a collection and my editor, Alice Major, applied her cartographical expertise with great skill, patience, and insight and drew the elusive map I'd been looking for all along.

I am also grateful for the encouragement from the sidelines along the way from Tim Cresswell, Barry Dempster, Clea Roberts, and Patricia Robertson, and am thankful for the financial nourishment provided by two Advanced Artist Awards from the Government of Yukon.

Some of these poems, or versions of them, have been published in journals and anthologies in Canada, the UK, and the US, namely: *Animal Chapbook, Arctica, Cutting Teeth, The Dalhousie Review, Dark Mountain: Issue Five, Dr. William Henry Drummond Poetry Contest Anthology, The Fiddlehead, Grain, Island, The Malahat Review, The Northern Review, Poetry About Love, Poetry and All That Jazz, PRISM international, Queen of the Sheep, subTerrain* and *The Walrus*.

I am delighted that some of the poems in the collection have embarked on their own journeys. "Night Vision" was adapted into a choral work by composer Stephen Chatman and consequently published, and a version of "Home" (called "Spring") was adapted into a choral work by composer Bruce Sled. "Folding" was selected by the Guernsey International Poetry Competition to appear on buses and at Guernsey airport. "Hope Stone II" was selected for the Fibre Art Network's exhibition *Ekphrastic* and interpreted by artists Beth Flemington, Vivian Kapusta, Pippa Moore, and Donna Stockdale. "The Gamekeeper" was displayed in London Art's *The Art of Love* exhibition on London's South Bank. "Hike" and "Behind the Houses" were published in a handmade book created by artist Joyce Majiski as part of her *North of Myth* exhibition.

A few of the poems were also finalists for and shortlisted in poetry contests and I am grateful for these boosts just as one appreciates a good meal and a hot shower to punctuate a long journey.

While I live in a different country from my family, who remain in England, they are with me always, especially my mother, Patricia, and eldest sister, Rebecca, whose own journeys ended too soon.

Finally, I thank my husband, Glenn, with whom I moved to Canada. As ever, I am grateful for his navigational skills and for always remembering to look back to check I'm not too far behind.